The Ultimate Nacho Experience

Over 100 Irresistible Recipes for Every Occasion. Discover the Perfect Combination of Crunchy Chips, Savory Toppings, and Bold Flavors to Create the Ultimate Nachos Experience

Kayden Bailey

Copyright Material ©2023

All Rights Reserved

Without the proper written consent of the publisher and copyright owner, this book cannot be used or distributed in any way, shape, or form, except for brief quotations used in a review. This book should not be considered a substitute for medical, legal, or other professional advice.

TABLE OF CONTENTS

TABLE OF CONTENTS 3
INTRODUCTION 7
BEEF NACHOS 8
   1. Classic Beef Nachos 9
   2. Camp Beef Nacho 11
   3. Fully Loaded Beef Nachos 13
   4. Tater tot nachos 15
   5. Grill nachos 17
   6. Retox Nachos 19
   7. Korean Beef Nachos 21
   8. BBQ Beef Nachos 23
   9. Spicy Beef Nachos 25
   10. Philly Cheese-steak Nachos 27
   11. Steak Nachos 29
   12. Beef and Bean Nachos 31
   13. Taco Beef Nachos 33
   14. Beef Fajita Nachos 35
CHICKEN NACHOS 37
   15. Loaded Chicken Nachos 38
   16. Nacho chicken casserole 40
   17. Buffalo Chicken Nachos 42
   18. Italian Nachos 44
   19. Chicken Fajita Nachos 47
   20. Classic Chicken Nachos 49
   21. BBQ Chicken Nachos 51
   22. Chicken Enchilada Nachos 53
   23. Chicken Guacamole Nachos 55

24. Chicken Taco Nachos 57
25. Chicken Chili Nachos 59
26. Chicken Bacon Ranch Nachos 61
27. Avocado Chicken Nachos 63
28. Greek Chicken Nachos 65
29. Teriyaki Chicken Nachos 67
30. Caprese Chicken Nachos 69
31. Korean BBQ Chicken Nachos 71

PORK NACHOS 73

32. Pulled Pork Nachos 74
33. Breakfast Bacon Nachos 76
34. Hawaiian Nachos 78
35. Honey-Lime Pork Nachos 80
36. Caribbean Nachos 82
37. Loaded BBQ Pork Nachos 84

VEGETABLE NACHOS 86

38. Vegetable and Cheddar Nachos 87
39. Vegetable Nachos 89
40. Sweet potato nachos 91
41. Loaded Potato Skin Nachos 93
42. Veggie Nachos 95
43. Greek Vegetable Nachos 97

BEAN NACHOS 99

44. Loaded Guacamole Nachos 100
45. Black Bean Tempeh Nachos with Cashew Cheese 102
46. Nachos with Avocado and Onion Microgreen 105
47. Cheesy Nachos 107
48. Hearty Nachos 109
49. Loaded Chili Nachos 112

50. Flax Chips Nachos 114

FISH AND SEAFOOD NACHOS 116

51. Shrimp Nachos 117
52. Crispy Prawns.. 119
53. Lobster Nachos.. 121
54. Tuna Nachos 123
55. Crab Nachos 125
56. Smoked Salmon Nachos.. 127
57. Fish Taco Nachos.. 129
58. Scallop Nachos.. 131
59. Shrimp and Crab Nachos 133
60. Ceviche Nachos.. 135

FRUIT AND DESSERT NACHOS 137

61. Apple nachos... 138
62. Gala nachos with mango-tequila sauce............................... 140
63. Nachos with mango-tequila sauce 142
64. Strawberry Cheesecake Nachos.. 144
65. Pineapple Coconut Nachos... 146
66. Chocolate Banana Nachos 148
67. Mango Salsa Nachos 150
68. Kiwi Lime Nachos.. 152
69. Berry Nutella Nachos... 154
70. Grilled Peach Nachos 156

NACHO DIPS.. 158

71. Brick Cheese Dip.. 159
72. Vegan Cannoli Dip... 161
73. Blue Cheese & Gouda Cheese Dip 163
74. Pub Cheese Dip.. 165
75. Spicy Corn Dip 167

76. Low-Carb pan pizza dip 169

77. Crab rangoon dip 171

78. Goat Cheese Guacamole 173

79. Bavarian party dip/spread 175

80. Baked artichoke party dip 177

81. Buffalo chicken dip 179

82. Ranch dip 181

83. Spicy shrimp and cheese dip 183

84. Garlic and bacon dip 185

85. Creamy Goat Cheese Pesto Dip 187

86. Hot Pizza Super dip 189

87. Baked Spinach and Artichoke Dip 191

88. Artichoke Dip 193

89. Creamy artichoke dip 195

90. Dill & Cream Cheese Dip 197

91. Wild rice and Chili Dip 199

92. Spicy Pumpkin & Cream Cheese Dip 201

93. Cream Cheese and Honey Dip 203

94. Creamy Spinach-Tahini Dip 205

95. Apricot And Chile Dipping Sauce 207

96. Roasted Eggplant Dip 209

97. Radish Microgreen & Lime Dip 212

98. Mango-Ponzu Dipping Sauce 214

99. Eggplant Walnut Spread 216

100. Sassy Spinach Dip With Roasted Garlic 218

CONCLUSION 220

INTRODUCTION

Welcome to the ultimate nachos cookbook, where you'll find everything you need to know to create the perfect plate of nachos for any occasion. Whether you're hosting a party, looking for a quick and easy snack, or just craving some delicious comfort food, nachos are the perfect choice.

In this book, you'll find over 100 irresistible nachos recipes that are sure to satisfy your cravings. From classic beef and cheese nachos to creative twists like BBQ chicken or loaded baked potato, there's something for everyone in these pages.

But it's not just about the toppings - we'll show you how to make your own homemade chips for the ultimate crispy crunch, as well as delicious sauces and dips to take your nachos to the next level. And with options for every dietary preference, including vegetarian and gluten-free, everyone can enjoy this delicious dish.

So get ready to discover the perfect combination of crunchy chips, savory toppings, and bold flavors to create the ultimate nachos experience. With our expert tips and tricks, you'll be whipping up mouthwatering nachos in no time. Let's get cooking!

nachos, cookbook, recipes, party, snack, comfort food, beef, cheese, BBQ chicken, loaded baked potato, homemade chips, crispy, crunch, sauces, dips, dietary preference, vegetarian, gluten-free, expert tips, mouthwatering.

BEEF NACHOS

1. <u>**Classic Beef Nachos**</u>

1 lb ground beef
1 packet of taco seasoning
1 bag of tortilla chips
2 cups of shredded cheddar cheese
1 cup of diced tomatoes
1 cup of diced onion
1 cup of salsa
1/2 cup of sliced jalapenos

Preheat the oven to 375°F. Brown the ground beef in a skillet and add the taco seasoning. Layer the tortilla chips on a baking sheet and top with the ground beef, cheese, tomatoes, onions, salsa, and jalapenos. Bake for 10-15 minutes or until the cheese is melted.

2. Camp Beef Nacho

- 1 lb Ground beef
- 1 lb Bulk, hot, pork sausage
- 2 lb Velveeta cheese, cubed
- 10 1/2 oz Cream of mushroom soup
- 10 1/2 oz Diced tomatoes and Green chilies, diced
- 2 ts Garlic powder
- 1 ts Black pepper

a) Brown the meat and sausage in a dutch oven; drain. Add remaining ingredients and heat until velveeta is melted. Mix well.
b) Continue heating until mixture is very warm. Serve with tortilla chips. Makes 8 cups of dip

3. **Fully Loaded Beef Nachos**

INGREDIENTS

- Ground beef (1-lbs, 0.45-kgs)
- 1 large bag tortilla chips
- 1 green bell pepper, seeded and diced
- Scallions, sliced – ½ cup
- Red onion, peeled and diced – ½ cup
- Cheddar cheese, shredded – 3 cups
- Sour cream, guacamole, salsa – to serve

Directions:

a) In a cast-iron pan, arrange a double layer of tortilla chips.
b) Scatter over the ground beef, bell pepper, scallions, red onion, and finally the cheddar cheese.
c) Place the cast-iron pan on the grill and cook for approximately 10 minutes until the cheese has melted completely.
d) Take off the grill and serve with sour cream, guacamole, and salsa on the side.

4. **Tater tot nachos**

SERVES: 2

INGREDIENTS
- 2 servings Tater Tots
- 6 oz. Ground Beef (80/20), cooked
- 2 oz. Cheddar Cheese, shredded
- 2 tbsp. Sour Cream
- 6 Black Olives, sliced
- 1 tbsp. Salsa
- 1/2 medium Jalapeno Pepper, sliced

DIRECTIONS
1. In a small casserole dish or mini cast iron skillet, lay down 9-10 tater tots.
2. Add 1/2 ground beef, and 1/2 of the shredded cheese. Start the second layer with fewer tater tots, 1/2 of the remaining beef, and 1/2 of the remaining cheese. Repeat with the last of the tater tots. Broil in the oven for 4-5 minutes so that the cheese melts.
3. Serve with jalapenos, sour cream, black olives, and salsa. Enjoy!

5. **Grill nachos**

Ingredient
- shredded cheese
- Tomatoes
- browned beef
- Salsa

Directions:
a) Simply line your griddle with aluminum foil and heap your nachos in. Add whatever you like on top,
b) Cover and Place in a moderate to low fire for a few minutes. Take out from fire when cheese is melted and serve.

6. **Retox Nachos**

Makes: 3 Servings

INGREDIENTS
- ½ avocado, diced
- 1 tablespoon extra-virgin olive oil
- 2 cups baby spinach
- ½ pound organic ground beef
- Sour cream, sliced jalapeños, fresh cilantro, for garnish
- Sesame blue tortilla chips
- 2 cloves garlic, minced
- ½ white onion, chopped
- 1 tomato, chopped

INSTRUCTIONS
a) Heat the oil in a pan over medium heat.
b) Cook garlic until it's golden.
c) Add spinach and cook until the spinach is wilted about 5 minutes.
d) Set aside.
e) Add ground beef to the same pan, breaking it up with a wooden spoon as it cooks.
f) When the meat is done, remove it from the pan and place it on top of the spinach.
g) Serve with onion, tomato, and avocado on top.
h) Garnish with sour cream, jalapenos, and cilantro.
i) Serve with tortilla chips.

7. **Korean Beef Nachos**

INGREDIENTS

1 lb. ground beef
2 tbsp. soy sauce
1 tbsp. brown sugar
1 tbsp. sesame oil
1/2 tsp. garlic powder
1/2 tsp. onion powder
1 bag tortilla chips
1 cup shredded cheddar cheese
1 cup shredded Monterey Jack cheese
1/4 cup sliced green onions
1/4 cup chopped fresh cilantro

INSTRUCTIONS

Preheat oven to 375°F.

In a skillet, brown the ground beef over medium-high heat. Drain any excess fat.

In a bowl, mix the soy sauce, brown sugar, sesame oil, garlic powder, and onion powder. Add the beef to the bowl and toss to coat.

On a baking sheet, spread out the tortilla chips in a single layer.

Sprinkle the shredded cheeses over the chips, then top with the beef mixture.

Bake for 10-15 minutes, or until the cheese is melted and bubbly.

Top with sliced green onions and chopped cilantro.

8. **BBQ Beef Nachos**

INGREDIENTS

1 lb. shredded cooked beef brisket or roast
1/2 cup BBQ sauce
1 bag tortilla chips
1 cup shredded cheddar cheese
1 cup shredded Monterey Jack cheese
1/4 cup diced red onion
1/4 cup chopped fresh cilantro
Sour cream for serving

INSTRUCTIONS

Preheat oven to 375°F.

In a bowl, mix the shredded beef with the BBQ sauce.

On a baking sheet, spread out the tortilla chips in a single layer.

Sprinkle the shredded cheeses over the chips, then top with the BBQ beef mixture.

Bake for 10-15 minutes, or until the cheese is melted and bubbly.

Top with diced red onion and chopped cilantro. Serve with sour cream.

9. **Spicy Beef Nachos**

INGREDIENTS

1 lb. ground beef
1 tbsp. chili powder
1 tsp. cumin
1/2 tsp. paprika
1/4 tsp. cayenne pepper
1/2 tsp. salt
1 bag tortilla chips
1 cup shredded cheddar cheese
1 cup shredded Monterey Jack cheese
1/4 cup diced jalapeño
1/4 cup chopped fresh cilantro

INSTRUCTIONS

Preheat oven to 375°F.

In a skillet, brown the ground beef over medium-high heat. Drain any excess fat.

In a bowl, mix the chili powder, cumin, paprika, cayenne pepper, and salt. Add the beef to the bowl and toss to coat.

On a baking sheet, spread out the tortilla chips in a single layer.

Sprinkle the shredded cheeses over the chips, then top with the beef mixture.

Bake for 10-15 minutes, or until the cheese is melted and bubbly.

Top with diced jalapeño and chopped cilantro.

10. Philly Cheese-steak Nachos

INGREDIENTS

1 lb. thinly sliced beef sirloin or flank steak
2 tbsp. olive oil
1 diced onion
1 diced green bell pepper
1/4 cup sliced mushrooms
1 bag tortilla chips
1 cup shredded provolone cheese
1/4 cup chopped fresh parsley

INSTRUCTIONS

Preheat oven to 375°F.
In a skillet, heat the olive oil over medium-high heat. Add the thinly sliced beef and cook until browned. Add the diced onion, green bell pepper, and sliced mushrooms and cook until softened.
On a baking sheet, spread out the tortilla chips in a single layer.
4. Sprinkle the shredded provolone cheese over the chips, then top with the beef mixture.

Bake for 10-15 minutes, or until the cheese is melted and bubbly.

Top with chopped fresh parsley.

11. Steak Nachos

INGREDIENTS

1 lb. grilled flank steak, thinly sliced
1 bag tortilla chips
1 cup shredded cheddar cheese
1 cup shredded Monterey Jack cheese
1/4 cup diced red onion
1/4 cup chopped fresh cilantro
Sour cream for serving

INSTRUCTIONS

Preheat oven to 375°F.

On a baking sheet, spread out the tortilla chips in a single layer.

Sprinkle the shredded cheeses over the chips, then top with the grilled flank steak.

Bake for 10-15 minutes, or until the cheese is melted and bubbly.

Top with diced red onion and chopped cilantro. Serve with sour cream.

12. **Beef and Bean Nachos**

INGREDIENTS

1 lb. ground beef
1 can black beans, drained and rinsed
1 tbsp. chili powder
1 tsp. cumin
1/2 tsp. paprika
1/4 tsp. cayenne pepper
1/2 tsp. salt
1 bag tortilla chips
1 cup shredded cheddar cheese
1 cup shredded Monterey Jack cheese
1/4 cup chopped fresh cilantro
Sour cream for serving

INSTRUCTIONS

Preheat oven to 375°F.

In a skillet, brown the ground beef over medium-high heat. Drain any excess fat.

Add the black beans, chili powder, cumin, paprika, cayenne pepper, and salt to the skillet. Stir to combine.

On a baking sheet, spread out the tortilla chips in a single layer.

Sprinkle the shredded cheeses over the chips, then top with the beef and bean mixture.

Bake for 10-15 minutes, or until the cheese is melted and bubbly.

Top with chopped fresh cilantro. Serve with sour cream.

13. Taco Beef Nachos

INGREDIENTS

1 lb. ground beef
1 tbsp. chili powder
1 tsp. cumin
1/2 tsp. paprika
1/4 tsp. cayenne pepper
1/2 tsp. salt
1 bag tortilla chips
1 cup shredded cheddar cheese
1 cup shredded Monterey Jack cheese
1/4 cup diced tomatoes
1/4 cup diced red onion
1/4 cup chopped fresh cilantro
Sour cream for serving

INSTRUCTIONS

Preheat oven to 375°F.

In a skillet, brown the ground beef over medium-high heat. Drain any excess fat.

Add the chili powder, cumin, paprika, cayenne pepper, and salt to the skillet. Stir to combine.

On a baking sheet, spread out the tortilla chips in a single layer.

Sprinkle the shredded cheeses over the chips, then top with the taco beef mixture.

Bake for 10-15 minutes, or until the cheese is melted and bubbly.

Top with diced tomatoes, diced red onion, and chopped cilantro. Serve with sour cream.

14. **Beef Fajita Nachos**

INGREDIENTS

1 lb. skirt steak, sliced
1 red bell pepper, sliced
1 green bell pepper, sliced
1/2 onion, sliced
1 bag tortilla chips
1 cup shredded cheddar cheese
1/4 cup chopped fresh cilantro
Sour cream for serving

INSTRUCTIONS

Preheat oven to 375°F.
In a skillet, cook the skirt steak over medium-high heat until browned. Remove from the skillet and set aside.
In the same skillet, cook the red and green bell peppers and onion until softened.
On a baking sheet, spread out the tortilla chips in a single layer. Sprinkle the shredded cheddar cheese over the chips, then top with the beef and fajita pepper mixture.
Bake for 10-15 minutes, or until the cheese is melted and bubbly.
Top with chopped fresh cilantro. Serve with sour cream.

CHICKEN NACHOS

15. Loaded Chicken Nachos

2 cups of cooked and shredded chicken
1 bag of tortilla chips
2 cups of shredded cheddar cheese
1 can of black beans
1/2 cup of diced red onion
1/2 cup of diced red bell pepper
1/2 cup of diced green bell pepper
1/4 cup of chopped cilantro
1/4 cup of sour cream

Layer the tortilla chips on a baking sheet and top with the shredded chicken, cheese, black beans, red onion, red bell pepper, green bell pepper, and cilantro. Bake for 10-15 minutes or until the cheese is melted. Top with sour cream before serving.

16. Nacho chicken casserole

INGREDIENTS
- .75 lbs. Chicken Thighs, boneless skinless
- 1 1/2 tsp. Chili seasoning
- 2 tbsp. Olive Oil
- 4 oz. Cream Cheese
- 4 oz. Cheddar Cheese
- 1 cup Green Chilies and Tomatoes
- 3 tbsp. Parmesan Cheese (~45g)
- 1/4 cup Sour Cream
- 16 oz. package Frozen Cauliflower
- 1 medium Jalapeno Pepper
- Salt and Pepper to Taste

DIRECTIONS

1. Pre-heat oven to 375F. Using kitchen shears, chop chicken into bite-size chunks. Season chicken with salt, pepper, and chili seasoning.
2. Over medium-high heat, cook chicken in olive oil until browned on all sides.
3. Add cream cheese, sour cream and 3/4 of the cheddar cheese to the chic-ken, and then stir together until melted and mixed. Add tomatoes and green chili and mix well.
4. In a casserole dish, add chicken mixture from the pan.
5. Microwave frozen cauliflower until cooked through. Use an immersion blender to blend with remaining cheese into a mashed potato-like consistency. Season with salt and pepper.
6. Cut a jalapeno into chunks. Spread cauliflower mixture over the top of the casserole, and then sprinkle jalapeno pepper over the top. Bake for 15-20 minutes or until some color is on the top and the jalapenos are cooked.
7. Slice and serve. Some fresh chopped cilantro tastes great over the top!

17. Buffalo Chicken Nachos

2 cups of cooked and shredded chicken
1 bag of tortilla chips
2 cups of shredded Monterey Jack cheese
1/2 cup of buffalo sauce
1/4 cup of chopped cilantro
1/4 cup of diced celery
Layer the tortilla chips on a baking sheet and top with the shredded chicken, shredded cheese, buffalo sauce, cilantro, and celery. Bake for 10-15 minutes or until the cheese is melted.

18. Italian Nachos

Makes: 1

INGREDIENTS
ALFREDO SAUCE
- 1 Cup Half and Half
- 1 Cup Heavy Cream
- 2 tablespoons unsalted butter
- 2 Cloves garlic minced
- ½ Cup Parmesan
- Salt and Pepper
- 2 Tablespoons flour

NACHOS
- Wonton wrappers cut in triangles
- 1 Chicken cooked and shredded
- Sautéed Peppers
- Mozzarella Cheese
- Olives
- Parsley chopped
- Parmesan Cheese
- Oil for frying peanut or canola

INSTRUCTIONS

a) Add the unsalted butter to a sauce saucepan and melt over medium heat.
b) Stir in the garlic until all of the butter has melted.
c) Add the flour quickly and whisk constantly until it is clumped together and golden.
d) In a mixing bowl, combine the heavy cream and half-and-half.
e) Bring to a boil, then reduce to a low heat and cook for 8-10 minutes, or until thickened.
f) Season with salt and pepper.
g) Wontons: Heat the oil in a big skillet over medium high heat, about ⅓ of the way up.
h) Add the wontons one at a time and heat until barely golden on the bottom, then flip and cook the other side.
i) Place a paper towel over the drain.
j) Preheat oven to 350°F and line a baking sheet with parchment paper, followed by the wontons.
k) Add Alfredo sauce, chicken, peppers, and mozzarella cheese on the top.
l) Place under the broiler in your oven for 5-8 minutes, or until the cheese is thoroughly melted.
m) Take out of the oven and top with olives, parmesan, and parsley.

19. Chicken Fajita Nachos

INGREDIENTS

2 chicken breasts, thinly sliced
2 tbsp. olive oil
1 diced onion
1 diced green bell pepper
1 bag tortilla chips
1 cup shredded cheddar cheese
1 cup shredded Monterey Jack cheese
1 diced tomato
1/4 cup chopped fresh cilantro
Sour cream for serving

INSTRUCTIONS

Preheat oven to 375°F.

In a skillet, heat the olive oil over medium-high heat. Add the thinly sliced chicken breasts and cook until browned. Add the diced onion and green bell pepper and cook until softened.

On a baking sheet, spread out the tortilla chips in a single layer.

Sprinkle the chicken mixture over the chips, then top with the shredded cheeses and diced tomato.

Bake for 10-15 minutes, or until the cheese is melted and bubbly.

Top with chopped cilantro and serve with sour cream.

20. Classic Chicken Nachos

INGREDIENTS
2 cups cooked shredded chicken
1 bag tortilla chips
1 cup shredded cheddar cheese
1 cup shredded Monterey Jack cheese
1/4 cup diced tomatoes
1/4 cup diced red onion
1/4 cup chopped fresh cilantro
Sour cream for serving
INSTRUCTIONS

Preheat oven to 375°F.

On a baking sheet, spread out the tortilla chips in a single layer.

Sprinkle the shredded cheeses over the chips, then top with the cooked shredded chicken.

Bake for 10-15 minutes, or until the cheese is melted and bubbly.

Top with diced tomatoes, diced red onion, and chopped cilantro. Serve with sour cream.

21.   BBQ Chicken Nachos

INGREDIENTS

2 cups cooked shredded chicken
1/2 cup BBQ sauce
1 bag tortilla chips
1 cup shredded cheddar cheese
1/4 cup diced red onion
1/4 cup chopped fresh cilantro
Ranch dressing for serving

INSTRUCTIONS

Preheat oven to 375°F.

In a bowl, mix the cooked shredded chicken with the BBQ sauce.

On a baking sheet, spread out the tortilla chips in a single layer.

Sprinkle the shredded cheddar cheese over the chips, then top with the BBQ chicken mixture.

Bake for 10-15 minutes, or until the cheese is melted and bubbly.

Top with diced red onion and chopped cilantro. Serve with ranch dressing.

22. <u>**Chicken Enchilada Nachos**</u>

INGREDIENTS

2 cups cooked shredded chicken
1 can (10 oz.) red enchilada sauce
1 bag tortilla chips
1 cup shredded cheddar cheese
1/4 cup diced red onion
1/4 cup chopped fresh cilantro
Sour cream for serving

INSTRUCTIONS

Preheat oven to 375°F.

In a bowl, mix the cooked shredded chicken with the red enchilada sauce.

On a baking sheet, spread out the tortilla chips in a single layer.

Sprinkle the shredded cheddar cheese over the chips, then top with the chicken and enchilada sauce mixture.

Bake for 10-15 minutes, or until the cheese is melted and bubbly.

Top with diced red onion and chopped fresh cilantro. Serve with sour cream.

23. Chicken Guacamole Nachos

INGREDIENTS

2 cups cooked shredded chicken
1/2 cup guacamole
1 bag tortilla chips
1 cup shredded Monterey Jack cheese
1/4 cup diced tomatoes
1/4 cup diced red onion
Sour cream for serving

INSTRUCTIONS

Preheat oven to 375°F.

On a baking sheet, spread out the tortilla chips in a single layer.

Sprinkle the shredded Monterey Jack cheese over the chips, then top with the cooked shredded chicken.

Bake for 10-15 minutes, or until the cheese is melted and bubbly.

Top with dollops of guacamole, diced tomatoes, and diced red onion. Serve with sour cream.

24. Chicken Taco Nachos

INGREDIENTS

2 cups cooked shredded chicken
1 packet taco seasoning
1 bag tortilla chips
1 cup shredded cheddar cheese
1/4 cup diced tomatoes
1/4 cup diced red onion
Sour cream for serving

INSTRUCTIONS

Preheat oven to 375°F.

In a bowl, mix the cooked shredded chicken with the taco seasoning.

On a baking sheet, spread out the tortilla chips in a single layer.

Sprinkle the shredded cheddar cheese over the chips, then top with the chicken and taco seasoning mixture.

Bake for 10-15 minutes, or until the cheese is melted and bubbly.

Top with diced tomatoes and diced red onion. Serve with sour cream.

25. Chicken Chili Nachos

INGREDIENTS

2 cups cooked shredded chicken
1 can (15 oz.) chili with beans
1 bag tortilla chips
1 cup shredded cheddar cheese
1/4 cup diced red onion
Sour cream for serving

INSTRUCTIONS

Preheat oven to 375°F.

In a saucepan, heat up the chili with beans.

On a baking sheet, spread out the tortilla chips in a single layer.

Sprinkle the shredded cheddar cheese over the chips, then top with the cooked shredded chicken.

Pour the heated chili with beans over the chicken and cheese.

Bake for 10-15 minutes, or until the cheese is melted and bubbly.

Top with diced red onion. Serve with sour cream.

26. Chicken Bacon Ranch Nachos

INGREDIENTS

2 cups cooked shredded chicken
1/2 cup ranch dressing
1 bag tortilla chips
1 cup shredded cheddar cheese
1/4 cup crumbled bacon
1/4 cup chopped fresh parsley

INSTRUCTIONS

Preheat oven to 375°F.
In a bowl, mix the cooked shredded chicken with the ranch dressing.
On a baking sheet, spread out the tortilla chips in a single layer. Sprinkle the shredded cheddar cheese over the chips, then top with the chicken and ranch dressing mixture.
5. Sprinkle the crumbled bacon over the top.

Bake for 10-15 minutes, or until the cheese is melted and bubbly.

Top with chopped fresh parsley.

27. Avocado Chicken Nachos

INGREDIENTS

2 cups cooked shredded chicken
1 bag tortilla chips
1 cup shredded pepper jack cheese
1 avocado, diced
1/4 cup diced red onion
1/4 cup chopped fresh cilantro
Lime wedges for serving

INSTRUCTIONS

Preheat oven to 375°F.

On a baking sheet, spread out the tortilla chips in a single layer.

Sprinkle the shredded pepper jack cheese over the chips, then top with the cooked shredded chicken.

Bake for 10-15 minutes, or until the cheese is melted and bubbly.

Top with diced avocado, diced red onion, and chopped fresh cilantro.

Serve with lime wedges on the side.

28.   Greek Chicken Nachos

INGREDIENTS

2 cups cooked shredded chicken
1 bag pita chips
1 cup crumbled feta cheese
1/2 cup diced cucumber
1/4 cup diced red onion
1/4 cup chopped Kalamata olives
1/4 cup chopped fresh parsley
1/4 cup tzatziki sauce for serving

INSTRUCTIONS

Preheat oven to 375°F.
On a baking sheet, spread out the pita chips in a single layer.
Sprinkle the crumbled feta cheese over the chips, then top with the cooked shredded chicken.
Bake for 10-15 minutes, or until the cheese is melted and bubbly.
Top with diced cucumber, diced red onion, chopped Kalamata olives, and chopped fresh parsley.
Serve with tzatziki sauce on the side.

29. Teriyaki Chicken Nachos

INGREDIENTS

2 cups cooked shredded chicken
1/4 cup teriyaki sauce
1 bag tortilla chips
1 cup shredded Monterey Jack cheese
1/4 cup diced green onion
Sesame seeds for serving

INSTRUCTIONS

Preheat oven to 375°F.

In a bowl, mix the cooked shredded chicken with the teriyaki sauce.

On a baking sheet, spread out the tortilla chips in a single layer.

Sprinkle the shredded Monterey Jack cheese over the chips, then top with the chicken and teriyaki sauce mixture.

Bake for 10-15 minutes, or until the cheese is melted and bubbly.

Top with diced green onion and sesame seeds.

30. Caprese Chicken Nachos

INGREDIENTS

2 cups cooked shredded chicken
1 bag pita chips
1 cup shredded mozzarella cheese
1 tomato, diced
1/4 cup chopped fresh basil
Balsamic glaze for serving

INSTRUCTIONS

Preheat oven to 375°F.

On a baking sheet, spread out the pita chips in a single layer.

Sprinkle the shredded mozzarella cheese over the chips, then top with the cooked shredded chicken.

Bake for 10-15 minutes, or until the cheese is melted and bubbly.

Top with diced tomato and chopped fresh basil.

Drizzle with balsamic glaze before serving.

31. Korean BBQ Chicken Nachos

INGREDIENTS

2 cups cooked shredded chicken
1/4 cup Korean BBQ sauce
1 bag tortilla chips
1 cup shredded pepper jack cheese
1/4 cup diced red onion
1/4 cup chopped fresh cilantro
Sriracha mayo for serving

INSTRUCTIONS

Preheat oven to 375°F.

In a bowl, mix the cooked shredded chicken with the Korean BBQ sauce.

On a baking sheet, spread out the tortilla chips in a single layer.

Sprinkle the shredded pepper jack cheese over the chips, then top with the chicken and Korean BBQ sauce mixture.

Bake for 10-15 minutes, or until the cheese is melted and bubbly.

Top with diced red onion and chopped fresh cilantro.

Drizzle with sriracha mayo before serving.

PORK NACHOS

32. **Pulled Pork Nachos**

2 cups of cooked and shredded pulled pork
1 bag of tortilla chips
2 cups of shredded Monterey Jack cheese
1 cup of BBQ sauce
1/2 cup of diced red onion
1/2 cup of diced pineapple
1/4 cup of chopped cilantro
Layer the tortilla chips on a baking sheet and top with the pulled pork, cheese, BBQ sauce, red onion, and pineapple. Bake for 10-15 minutes or until the cheese is melted. Top with cilantro before serving.

33. Breakfast Bacon Nachos

1 bag of tortilla chips
2 cups of shredded cheddar cheese
4 scrambled eggs
4 slices of cooked bacon, chopped
1/2 cup of diced tomato
1/4 cup of chopped green onion
1/4 cup of sour cream
Layer the tortilla chips on a baking sheet and top with the shredded cheese, scrambled eggs, chopped bacon, diced tomato, and green onion. Bake for 10-15 minutes or until the cheese is melted. Top with sour cream before serving.

34. Hawaiian Nachos

1 bag of tortilla chips
2 cups of shredded mozzarella cheese
1 cup of diced ham
1 cup of diced pineapple
1/2 cup of diced red onion
1/4 cup of chopped cilantro

Layer the tortilla chips on a baking sheet and top with the shredded mozzarella cheese, diced ham, diced pineapple, red onion, and cilantro. Bake for 10-15 minutes or until the cheese is melted.

35. Honey-Lime Pork Nachos

Makes: 8

INGREDIENTS
- 1½ pounds boneless pork loin, trimmed
- 1¼ teaspoons kosher salt
- 3 tablespoons honey
- 3 tablespoons fresh lime juice
- 1 tablespoon sliced garlic
- 8 ounces baked multigrain tortilla chips
- 4 ounces pepper Jack cheese, shredded
- ½ cup diced tomato
- ⅓ cup thinly sliced red onion
- ¼ cup chopped fresh cilantro
- ⅓ cup reduced-fat sour cream
- 2 tablespoons whole milk
- 8 lime wedges

INSTRUCTIONS
a) Sprinkle the pork with 1 teaspoon of salt, and place in a Crockpot. Drizzle with honey and lime juice; top with the garlic slices.
b) Slow cook until a thermometer inserted in the thickest part of the pork registers 140°F, 2 to 3 hours.
c) Transfer the pork to a cutting board, reserving the drippings in the Crockpot; let the pork rest for 10 minutes. Cut the pork into small cubes, and toss with the reserved drippings in the Crockpot.
d) Arrange the chips in an even layer on a rimmed baking sheet, and top with the pork and cheese.
e) Broil until the cheese is melted, about 4 minutes. Top with the tomato, onion, cilantro, and remaining ¼ teaspoon salt.
f) Combine sour cream and milk, and drizzle over the nachos.
g) Serve with lime wedges.

36. Caribbean Nachos

Ingredients

- 1 (16-ounce) package tortilla chips
- 1 red bell pepper, diced
- 1 bunch green onions, chopped
- 1 avocado - peeled, pitted, and diced
- 1/2 pineapple, peeled and cut
- 8 thick slices bacon
- 3/4 cup Caribbean jerk marinade
- 1 pound cooked shrimp, peeled
- 1/2 pound Monterey jack cheese

Directions

a) Layer the chips on a tray or cookie sheet. Arrange the red pepper, orange pepper, onion, avocado, and pineapple combined with the chips.
b) Place bacon in a big, deep skillet. Cook over medium-high heat until evenly crisp; drain on a plate lined with paper towels.
c) Pour the jerk marinade in to a saucepan over medium heat. Cook, stirring continually, before marinade reduces to a thick sticky consistency, around three minutes. Add the shrimp and stir to coat; cook before shrimp are hot. Scatter the shrimp over the nachos; top with Monterrey Jack cheese and cilantro.
d) Place the nachos in the oven before cheese is melted, about 7 minutes.

37. Loaded BBQ Pork Nachos

INGREDIENTS

2 cups shredded cooked pork
1/4 cup barbecue sauce
1 bag tortilla chips
1 cup shredded cheddar cheese
1 cup shredded Monterey Jack cheese
1 diced red onion
1/4 cup chopped fresh cilantro
Sour cream for serving

INSTRUCTIONS

Preheat oven to 375°F.

In a bowl, mix the shredded pork with the barbecue sauce until coated.

On a baking sheet, spread out the tortilla chips in a single layer.

Sprinkle the pulled pork over the chips, then top with the shredded cheeses and diced red onion.

Bake for 10-15 minutes, or until the cheese is melted and bubbly.

Top with fresh cilantro and serve with sour cream.

VEGETABLE NACHOS

38. <u>Vegetable and Cheddar Nachos</u>

1 bag of tortilla chips
2 cups of shredded cheddar cheese
1 can of black beans
1 diced red bell pepper
1 diced green bell pepper
1/2 cup of diced onion
1/2 cup of diced tomato
1/4 cup of chopped cilantro

Layer the tortilla chips on a baking sheet and top with the shredded cheese, black beans, red bell pepper, green bell pepper, onion, and tomato. Bake for 10-15 minutes or until the cheese is melted. Top with cilantro before serving.

39. Vegetable Nachos

Servings: 3

INGREDIENTS
- 8 ounces Tortilla chips
- ½ cup Grilled chicken
- 1 can Black beans, drained, rinsed
- 1 cup White queso
- ½ cup Grape tomatoes, halved
- ⅓ cup Green onion, diced

Directions:
1. Use foil to line the air fry basket.
2. Using a nonstick spray, coat the surface.
3. Assemble the nachos by layering the chips, chicken, and beans on top.
4. Place a layer of queso on top.
5. Add tomatoes and onions to the top.
6. Turn on Ninja Foodi Digital Air Fryer Oven and rotate the knob to select "Air Fry".
7. Select the timer for 5 minutes and the temperature for 355 °F.
8. Remove from Ninja Foodi Digital Air Fryer Oven to serve.

40. Sweet potato nachos

Makes: 6

INGREDIENTS
- 1 tablespoon olive oil
- ⅓ cup chopped tomato
- ⅓ cup chopped avocado
- 1 teaspoon chili powder
- 1 teaspoon garlic powder
- 3 sweet potatoes
- 1½ teaspoons paprika
- ⅓ cup reduced-fat shredded Cheddar cheese

INSTRUCTIONS
a) Preheat oven to 425 degrees Fahrenheit. Coat the baking pans with nonstick cooking spray and cover them with foil.
b) Peel and thinly slice the sweet potatoes into 14-inch rounds.
c) Toss the rounds with olive oil, chili powder, garlic powder, and paprika.
d) Spread equally on the preheated pan and bake for 25 minutes, flipping halfway through the cooking time until crisp.
e) Remove the skillet from the oven and top the sweet potatoes with beans and cheese.
f) Bake for another 2 minutes until the cheese has melted.
g) Toss in the tomato and avocado. Serve.

41. Loaded Potato Skin Nachos

INGREDIENTS

4 russet potatoes
2 tbsp. olive oil
1 bag tortilla chips
1 cup shredded cheddar cheese
1 cup shredded Monterey Jack cheese
6 strips cooked bacon, crumbled
1/4 cup sliced green onions
1/4 cup sour cream

INSTRUCTIONS

Preheat oven to 375°F.

Wash and dry the potatoes, then prick with a fork all over. Rub with olive oil and place on a baking sheet. Bake for 45-60 minutes, or until tender.

Cut the potatoes in half lengthwise and scoop out the flesh, leaving a thin layer of potato in the skins.

On a baking sheet, spread out the tortilla chips in a single layer. Place the potato skins on top of the chips.

Sprinkle the shredded cheeses and crumbled bacon over the potato skins and chips.

Bake for 10-15 minutes, or until the cheese is melted and bubbly.

Top with sliced green onions and dollops of sour cream.

42. <u>Veggie Nachos</u>

INGREDIENTS

1 can black beans, drained and rinsed
1 can corn, drained
1 bag tortilla chips
1 cup shredded cheddar cheese
1 cup shredded Monterey Jack cheese
1 diced tomato
1 diced jalapeño
1/4 cup sliced black olives
1/4 cup chopped fresh cilantro
Salsa, sour cream, and guacamole for serving

INSTRUCTIONS

Preheat oven to 375°F.
On a baking sheet, spread out the tortilla chips in a single layer.
Spiinkle the black beans and corn over the chips, then top with the shredded cheeses, diced tomato, jalapeño, and black olives.
4. Bake for 10-15 minutes, or until the cheese is melted and bubbly.

Top with fresh cilantro and serve with salsa, sour cream, and guacamole.

43. Greek Vegetable Nachos

INGREDIENTS

1 bag pita chips
1 cup crumbled feta cheese
1 cup diced cucumber
1 cup diced tomato
1/4 cup sliced kalamata olives
1/4 cup chopped fresh parsley
Tzatziki sauce for serving

INSTRUCTIONS

Preheat oven to 375°F.
On a baking sheet, spread out the pita chips in a single layer.
Sprinkle the crumbled feta cheese over the chips, then top with the diced cucumber and tomato.
Sprinkle the sliced kalamata olives over the nachos.
Bake for 10-15 minutes, or until the cheese is melted and bubbly.
Top with chopped parsley and serve with tzatziki sauce.

BEAN NACHOS

44. Loaded Guacamole Nachos

INGREDIENTS

1 bag of tortilla chips
2 cups of shredded cheddar cheese
1 cup of black beans
1 cup of diced tomatoes
1/4 cup of chopped cilantro
1/4 cup of diced red onion
1/2 cup of sour cream
1/2 cup of guacamole

INSTRUCTIONS

Preheat the oven to 350°F (175°C).
Layer the tortilla chips on a baking sheet.
Sprinkle the shredded cheddar cheese over the tortilla chips.
Add the black beans and diced tomatoes over the cheese.
Bake in the oven for 10-15 minutes or until the cheese is melted.
Remove from the oven and top with chopped cilantro and diced red onion.
Drizzle the sour cream and guacamole over the top.
Serve and enjoy!

45. Black Bean Tempeh Nachos with Cashew Cheese

Yield: 4 servings

INGREDIENTS
Cashew Cheese
¾ cup raw cashews, soaked from 1 hour to overnight and drained
1 tablespoon nutritional yeast
1 tablespoon tapioca starch or tapioca flour (they are the same thing)
½ teaspoon garlic powder
½ teaspoon onion powder
1 tablespoon lemon juice
½ cup water
Tempeh Nachos
10 to 18 ounces tortilla chips
1 15-ounce can black beans, drained and rinsed
½ cup diced red onion
1 Roma tomato, diced small
Lettuce
8 ounces tempeh, diced very small
1 hot chili pepper, sliced thin crosswise
2 tablespoons raw shelled hempseed
1 avocado
Juice from one lime

INSTRUCTIONS

Cashew Cheese

1. Add all the cheese ingredients to a blender and blend until smooth. Transfer this blended mixture into a small saucepan. Cook on medium heat and stir until the sauce thickens a bit. It will take about 5 to 10 minutes. Take off the heat to cool slightly.

To Assemble the Nachos

2. Lay the lettuce and all the chips on a platter. Sprinkle black beans over the chips. Dot with cashew cheese. Sprinkle the red onion, tomato, tempeh, chili pepper, and hempseed all over the top.

3. Dice the avocado and dredge in lime juice. Sprinkle diced avocado over the nachos.

46. Nachos with Avocado and Onion Microgreen

Makes: 2

INGREDIENTS
- Sprouted wheat tortillas
- Avocado/guacamole
- Tomatoes
- Jalapeños, thinly sliced
- ½ can of kidney beans
- Handful onion microgreens

INSTRUCTIONS
a) To make the sprouted wheat tortillas crisp and warm, lightly toast them.
b) Mash the avocado with a fork and spread it on the tortillas.
c) Garnish with tomatoes, jalapeños, kidney beans, and onion microgreens.

47. Cheesy Nachos

INGREDIENTS

- 4 ounces of corn tortilla chips
- ½ cup salsa
- 1 cup of grated cheddar or jack cheese
- Colorful toppings such as baby spinach leaves, red kidney beans, corn kernels, cherry tomatoes, and sliced bell peppers

INSTRUCTIONS

a) Arrange the corn chips on a microwave-proof plate.
b) Spread the salsa over the corn chips.
c) Arrange the spinach, beans, corn, tomatoes, and peppers.
d) Sprinkle the cheese over it.
e) Microwave on high for 1½ minutes until the cheese is melted.
f) Serve with guacamole, sour cream, or extra salsa.

48. Hearty Nachos

SERVES 4

FOR THE "CHEESE" SAUCE:
½ cup raw cashews, soaked in warm water for at least 30 minutes, rinsed well
1 tablespoon tahini
1 red bell pepper, roasted and seeded
¼ cup nutritional yeast
1 tablespoon low-sodium soy sauce, or Bragg Liquid Aminos
Zest and juice of ½ lemon
¼ teaspoon cayenne pepper

FOR THE "REFRIED" BEAN DIP:
One 15-ounce can pinto beans, drained and rinsed
1 cup Fresh Tomato Salsa
1½ teaspoons chili powder

FOR THE NACHOS:
½ cup finely chopped cilantro, parsley, or lettuce
1 avocado, halved, pitted, peeled, and sliced, optional
½ cup Fresh Tomato Salsa
½ cup diced fresh tomatoes
Baked corn tortillas, cut into chips (see tip)

TO MAKE THE "CHEESE" SAUCE:
1. In a blender, combine the soaked cashews, tahini, roasted red pepper, nutritional yeast, soy sauce, lemon zest and juice, cayenne pepper, and ¼ cup water. Blend on high until smooth. Set aside.

TO MAKE THE "REFRIED" BEAN DIP:
2. Add the beans, salsa, and chili powder in the bowl of a food processor. Puree until smooth, adding water, as needed, to achieve a smooth consistency. Place the pureed beans in a medium saucepan and warm over low heat until heated through. Keep warm until ready to serve.

TO ASSEMBLE THE NACHOS:
3. Spread bean dip evenly onto the bottom of a medium-sized serving bowl or baking dish. Smooth the surface and sprinkle cilantro over beans. Pour the "cheese" sauce on top of the cilantro. Garnish with sliced avocado (if using), salsa, and diced fresh tomatoes and serve with the baked corn chips.

49. Loaded Chili Nachos

1 can of chili
1 bag of tortilla chips
2 cups of shredded cheddar cheese
1/2 cup of diced tomato
1/4 cup of chopped cilantro
1/4 cup of diced red onion
Layer the tortilla chips on a baking sheet and top with the chili, shredded cheese, diced tomato, cilantro, and red onion. Bake for 10-15 minutes or until the cheese is melted.

50. Flax Chips Nachos

INGREDIENTS
1 recipe Salted Flax Chips
1 recipe Taco Nut Meat
1 recipe Chipotle Cheese
1 recipe Heirloom Tomato Salsa
1 ripe avocado, pitted and diced

INSTRUCTIONS
Assemble your nachos by placing the Salted Flax Chips on a serving platter. Top with the taco meat, Cheese, salsa, and avocado. Enjoy immediately.

FISH AND SEAFOOD NACHOS

51. Shrimp Nachos

1 lb cooked and peeled shrimp
1 bag of tortilla chips
2 cups of shredded cheddar cheese
1 diced avocado
1/2 cup of diced tomato
1/4 cup of chopped cilantro
1/4 cup of diced red onion

Layer the tortilla chips on a baking sheet and top with the cooked shrimp, shredded cheese, diced avocado, diced tomato, cilantro, and red onion. Bake for 10-15 minutes or until the cheese is melted.

52. Crispy Prawns

Servings: 4

INGREDIENTS
1 egg
½ pound nacho chips, crushed
12 prawns, peeled and deveined

Directions:
1. In a shallow dish, beat the egg.
2. In another shallow dish, place the crushed nacho chips.
3. Coat the prawn with the beaten egg and then roll into nacho chips.
4. Press AIR OVEN MODE button of Ninja Foodi Digital Air Fryer Oven and turn the dial to select "Air Fry" mode.
5. Press TIME/SLICES button and again turn the dial to set the cooking time to 8 minutes.
6. Now push TEMP/SHADE button and rotate the dial to set the temperature at 355 °F.
7. Press "Start/Stop" button to start.
8. When the unit beeps to show that it is preheated, open the oven door.
9. Arrange the prawns into the air fry basket and insert in the oven.
10. When cooking time is completed, open the oven door and serve immediately.

53. <u>**Lobster Nachos**</u>

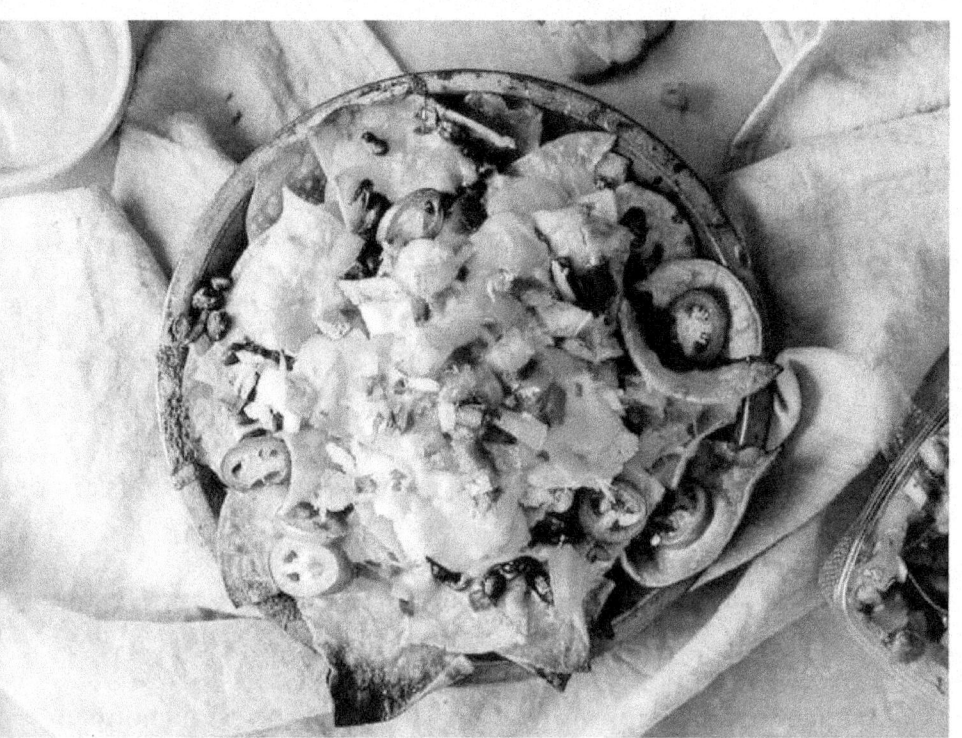

INGREDIENTS

1 lb cooked lobster meat, chopped
1 tbsp butter
1 tbsp flour
1 cup milk
Salt and pepper
Tortilla chips
1 cup shredded Monterey Jack cheese
Chopped fresh parsley

INSTRUCTIONS

Preheat the oven to 350°F.

In a saucepan over medium heat, melt the butter and whisk in the flour. Cook for 1-2 minutes.

Gradually whisk in the milk until smooth. Season with salt and pepper.

Arrange tortilla chips on a baking sheet and top with chopped lobster meat and shredded cheese.

Pour the sauce over the nachos and bake in the oven for 8-10 minutes, or until the cheese is melted and bubbly.

Garnish with chopped parsley.

54.   <u>Tuna Nachos</u>

INGREDIENTS

1 can of tuna, drained and flaked
1 tbsp olive oil
1 tsp cumin
1 tsp chili powder
Salt and pepper
Tortilla chips
1 cup shredded Pepper Jack cheese
Sliced green onions

INSTRUCTIONS

Preheat the oven to 350°F.

In a bowl, toss the tuna with olive oil, cumin, chili powder, salt, and pepper.

Arrange tortilla chips on a baking sheet and top with shredded cheese and the seasoned tuna.

Bake in the oven for 8-10 minutes, or until the cheese is melted and bubbly.

Garnish with sliced green onions.

55. **Crab Nachos**

INGREDIENTS

1 lb crab meat
1 tbsp butter
1 tbsp flour
1 cup milk
Salt and pepper
Tortilla chips
1 cup shredded cheddar cheese
Chopped fresh cilantro

INSTRUCTIONS

Preheat the oven to 350°F.

In a saucepan over medium heat, melt the butter and whisk in the flour. Cook for 1-2 minutes.

Gradually whisk in the milk until smooth. Season with salt and pepper.

Arrange tortilla chips on a baking sheet and top with the crab meat and shredded cheese.

Pour the sauce over the nachos and bake in the oven for 8-10 minutes, or until the cheese is melted and bubbly.

Garnish with chopped cilantro.

56. Smoked Salmon Nachos

INGREDIENTS

4 oz smoked salmon, chopped
4 oz cream cheese, softened
1 tbsp capers
1 tbsp chopped fresh dill
Salt and pepper
Tortilla chips
1 cup shredded mozzarella cheese

INSTRUCTIONS

Preheat the oven to 350°F.
In a bowl, mix the smoked salmon, cream continue
cheese, capers, dill, salt, and pepper until well combined.
3. Arrange tortilla chips on a baking sheet and top with the smoked salmon mixture and shredded mozzarella cheese.

Bake in the oven for 8-10 minutes, or until the cheese is melted and bubbly.

57. <u>**Fish Taco Nachos**</u>

INGREDIENTS

1 lb white fish (such as cod), cut into small pieces
2 tbsp olive oil
1 tbsp chili powder
Salt and pepper
Tortilla chips
1 cup shredded Pepper Jack cheese
Chopped fresh cilantro
Sliced avocado

INSTRUCTIONS

Preheat the oven to 350°F.

In a bowl, toss the fish with olive oil, chili powder, salt, and pepper.

Arrange tortilla chips on a baking sheet and top with shredded cheese and the seasoned fish.

Bake in the oven for 8-10 minutes, or until the cheese is melted and bubbly.

Garnish with chopped cilantro and sliced avocado.

58. **Scallop Nachos**

INGREDIENTS

1 lb sea scallops
2 tbsp olive oil
2 cloves garlic, minced
Salt and pepper
Tortilla chips
1 cup shredded Monterey Jack cheese
Sliced jalapeños

INSTRUCTIONS

Preheat the oven to 350°F.

In a pan over medium heat, cook the scallops with olive oil and garlic until browned and cooked through. Season with salt and pepper.

Arrange tortilla chips on a baking sheet and top with shredded cheese and the cooked scallops.

Bake in the oven for 8-10 minutes, or until the cheese is melted and bubbly.

Garnish with sliced jalapeños.

59. **Shrimp and Crab Nachos**

INGREDIENTS

1 lb shrimp, peeled and deveined
1 lb crab meat
2 cloves garlic, minced
Tortilla chips
1 cup shredded cheddar cheese
Chopped fresh parsley

INSTRUCTIONS

Preheat the oven to 350°F.

In a pan over medium heat, cook the shrimp and garlic until pink and cooked through. Set aside.

Arrange tortilla chips on a baking sheet and top with the cooked shrimp, crab meat, and shredded cheese.

Bake in the oven for 8-10 minutes, or until the cheese is melted and bubbly.

Garnish with chopped parsley.

60. Ceviche Nachos

INGREDIENTS

1 lb white fish (such as tilapia or snapper), diced
1/2 cup lime juice
1/4 cup orange juice
1/4 cup chopped cilantro
1/4 cup diced red onion
Salt and pepper
Tortilla chips
1 cup shredded Monterey Jack cheese

INSTRUCTIONS

In a bowl, combine the fish, lime juice, orange juice, cilantro, red onion, salt, and pepper. Let marinate in the fridge for 30 minutes to an hour.

Preheat the oven to 350°F.

Arrange tortilla chips on a baking sheet and top with the marinated fish and shredded cheese.

Bake in the oven for 8-10 minutes, or until the cheese is melted and bubbly.

FRUIT AND DESSERT NACHOS

61. Apple nachos

Makes: For 1

INGREDIENTS
- 2 apples of your choice
- ⅓ cup natural nut butter
- a small handful of grated coconut
- Sprinkle cinnamon
- 1 tablespoon lemon juice

INSTRUCTIONS
a) Apples: Wash, core, and cut your apples into ¼-inch slices.
b) Put the apple slices in a small bowl with the lemon juice and toss.
c) Nut Butter: Heat your nut butter until warm and slightly runny.
d) Drizzle the nut butter in a circular motion from the center of the plate to the outer edge.
e) Sprinkle with coconut flakes and sprinkle with cinnamon.

62. Gala nachos with mango-tequila sauce

Yield: 6 servings

Ingredient
- 6 Corn OR 4 Flour tortillas
- 3 tablespoons Butter
- 6 tablespoons Sugar up to
- 1½ quart Ice cream or sherbet or a mixture
- 3 cups Cut fresh fruit
- Mango-Tequila Sauce;
- Sugared Nuts
- ¾ cup Chocolate chips

Directions:

a) Stack the tortillas in one pile and cut into triangles, 6 each for corn, or 8 each for flour.

b) Place ½ tablespoon of the butter and 1 tablespoon of the sugar in a large frying pan. Set over medium heat until the butter foams and the sugar melts.

c) Add as many tortilla triangles as will fit without overlapping and fry until they puff up, about 1 minute. Turn and fry on the other side until golden, about 1 minute more. Remove to a plate without overlapping. Add more butter and sugar to the pan and continue more rounds until all of the triangles are crisped.

d) To assemble, arrange scoops of ice cream or sherbet in the center of a large platter. Strew fruit pieces around the ice cream and tuck tortilla triangles in here and there. Spoon Mango-Tequila sauce over all. Dot with Sugared Nuts and chocolate chips. Serve right away.

63. Nachos with mango-tequila sauce

Makes: 6 servings

INGREDIENTS
- 6 Corn or 4 Flour tortillas
- 3 tablespoons Butter
- 6 tablespoons Sugar up to
- 1½ quart Ice cream or sherbet
- 3 cups Cut fresh fruit

MANGO-TEQUILA SAUCE:
- Sugared Nuts
- ¾ cup Chocolate chips

INSTRUCTIONS
e) Stack the tortillas in one pile and cut into triangles, 6 each for corn, or 8 each for flour.

f) Place ½ tablespoon of the butter and 1 tablespoon of the sugar in a large frying pan. Set over medium heat until the butter foams and the sugar melts.

g) Add as many tortilla triangles as will fit without overlapping and fry until they puff up, about 1 minute. Turn and fry on the other side until golden, about 1 minute more. Remove to a plate without overlapping. Add more butter and sugar to the pan and continue more rounds until all of the triangles are crisped.

h) To assemble, arrange scoops of ice cream or sherbet in the center of a large platter. Strew fruit pieces around the ice cream and tuck tortilla triangles in here and there. Spoon Mango-Tequila sauce over all. Dot with Sugared Nuts and chocolate chips. Serve right away.

64. Strawberry Cheesecake Nachos

INGREDIENTS

1 package cinnamon sugar tortilla chips
1 pint strawberries, diced
8 oz cream cheese, softened
1/2 cup powdered sugar
1 tsp vanilla extract
Whipped cream

INSTRUCTIONS

In a bowl, mix together the cream cheese, powdered sugar, and vanilla extract until smooth.

Arrange the tortilla chips on a platter and top with the diced strawberries and dollops of the cream cheese mixture.

Drizzle with whipped cream.

65. Pineapple Coconut Nachos

INGREDIENTS

1 package plain tortilla chips
1 can crushed pineapple, drained
1/2 cup shredded coconut
1/2 cup sweetened condensed milk
1 tsp vanilla extract

INSTRUCTIONS

Preheat the oven to 350°F.

Arrange the tortilla chips on a baking sheet and top with the crushed pineapple and shredded coconut.

Drizzle the sweetened condensed milk and vanilla extract over the top.

Bake in the oven for 8-10 minutes, or until the coconut is toasted and the milk is bubbly.

66. Chocolate Banana Nachos

INGREDIENTS

1 package chocolate tortilla chips
2 bananas, sliced
1/2 cup chocolate chips, melted
Chopped nuts (optional)

INSTRUCTIONS

Arrange the chocolate tortilla chips on a platter and top with the sliced bananas.

Drizzle the melted chocolate over the top.

Sprinkle with chopped nuts, if desired.

67. Mango Salsa Nachos

INGREDIENTS

1 package plain tortilla chips
2 mangoes, diced
1/4 cup diced red onion
1/4 cup chopped cilantro
1 jalapeño pepper, seeded and minced
Juice of 1 lime
Salt and pepper
INSTRUCTIONS

In a bowl, mix together the diced mangoes, red onion, cilantro, jalapeño pepper, lime juice, salt, and pepper.

Arrange the tortilla chips on a platter and top with the mango salsa.

68. Kiwi Lime Nachos

INGREDIENTS

1 package plain tortilla chips
4 kiwis, peeled and sliced
Juice of 2 limes
1/4 cup honey
INSTRUCTIONS

Arrange the tortilla chips on a platter and top with the sliced kiwis.

Drizzle the lime juice and honey over the top.

69. Berry Nutella Nachos

INGREDIENTS

1 package cinnamon sugar tortilla chips
1 cup mixed berries (such as strawberries, blueberries, and raspberries)
1/2 cup Nutella
Chopped nuts (optional)

INSTRUCTIONS

Arrange the cinnamon sugar tortilla chips on a platter and top with the mixed berries.

Microwave the Nutella for 15-20 seconds to soften it.

Drizzle the Nutella over the top.

Sprinkle with chopped nuts, if desired.

70. Grilled Peach Nachos

INGREDIENTS

1 package plain tortilla chips
3 peaches, halved and pitted
1/4 cup honey
1/4 cup balsamic vinegar
1/4 cup chopped fresh mint

INSTRUCTIONS

Preheat a grill to medium-high heat.
Grill the peach halves for 3-4 minutes per side, until slightly charred.
Arrange the tortilla chips on a platter and top with the grilled peach halves.
4. Drizzle the honey and balsamic vinegar over the top.

Sprinkle with chopped fresh mint.

NACHO DIPS

71. Brick Cheese Dip

Makes: 2 Servings

INGREDIENTS
- 3 oz ricotta cheese
- 3 oz freshly grated brick cheese
- 3 Tablespoons fresh thyme leaves
- 6 oz goat cheese
- 1 oz parmesan hard cheese, freshly grated
- 4 strips thick-cut bacon, cooked and crumbled
- Salt and pepper, to taste

INSTRUCTIONS
a) Prepare the oven for broiling.
b) Combine all of the ingredients in a baking dish.
c) Sprinkle the Parmesan cheese over the dish.
d) Bake in a preheated oven for 5 minutes, or until the cheese begins to brown and bubble.
e) Remove from the oven and serve immediately.

72. Vegan Cannoli Dip

Makes: 8

INGREDIENTS
- 3/4 cup Coconut milk, full-fat
- 8 oz Vegan cream cheese
- 1 tsp Almond extract, pure
- 3/4 cup Confectioners' sugar
- 1/2 tsp Vanilla extract
- 1 cup Almonds, raw
- 2 cups Cashews, raw
- 2 tbsp Pistachios

INSTRUCTIONS
a) Blend all the ingredients.

73. Blue Cheese & Gouda Cheese Dip

Makes: 2 Servings

INGREDIENTS
- 2 tablespoons unsalted butter
- 1 cup sweet onion, diced
- 2 cups cream cheese, at room temperature
- ⅛ teaspoon salt
- ⅛ teaspoon white pepper
- ⅓ cup Montucky Cold Snacks
- 1 ½ cups chopped fake chicken
- ½ cup honey mustard, plus more for drizzling
- 2 tablespoons ranch dressing
- 1 cup shredded cheddar cheese
- 2 cups Gouda cheese, shredded
- 2 tablespoons blue cheese dressing
- ⅓ cup crumbled blue cheese, plus more for topping
- ¾ cup honey BBQ sauce, plus more for drizzling

INSTRUCTIONS
a) In a large skillet, melt the butter over low heat.
b) Stir in the diced onions and season with salt and pepper.
c) Cook for 5 minutes, or until slightly softened.
d) Cook, stirring frequently, until the onions caramelize, about 25 to 30 minutes.
e) Preheat the oven to 375° F.
f) Coat a 9-inch baking dish with nonstick cooking spray.
g) Combine the cream cheese, all of the cheese, BBQ sauce, honey mustard, ranch dressing, and blue cheese in a large mixing bowl.
h) Add the caramelized onions and fake chicken.
i) Place the batter in a baking dish.
j) Garnish with the remaining cheese.
k) Bake the dip for 20–25 minutes, or until golden.
l) Serve immediately.

74. **Pub Cheese Dip**

Makes: 2 Servings

INGREDIENTS
- 3 tablespoons coarsely chopped, pickled jalapeno peppers
- 1 cup hard cider
- ⅛ teaspoon ground red pepper
- 2 cups shredded extra sharp, yellow cheddar cheese
- 2 cups shredded Colby Cheese
- 2 tablespoons cornstarch
- 1 tablespoon Dijon mustard
- 60 crackers

INSTRUCTIONS
- In a medium mixing bowl, combine cheddar cheese, Colby cheese, and cornstarch. Place aside.
- In a medium saucepan, combine cider and mustard.
- Cook until boiling over medium-high heat.
- Slowly whisk in the cheese mixture, a little at a time, until smooth.
- Turn off the heat.
- Stir in the jalapeno and red peppers.
- Place the mixture in a 1-quart slow cooker or fondue pot.
- Keep warm on low heat.
- Serve alongside crackers.

75. Spicy Corn Dip

Makes: 6 Servings

INGREDIENTS
- 1 tablespoon extra-virgin olive oil
- ½ pound spicy Italian sausage
- 1 medium red onion, diced
- 1 large red bell pepper, diced
- 1 cup sour cream
- 4 ounces of cream cheese, at room temperature
- 4 cups frozen corn, thawed
- ½ cup chopped green onions
- 1 large jalapeño, diced
- 4 garlic cloves, chopped
- 1 tablespoon chopped cilantro
- 2 teaspoons Creole seasoning
- 1 teaspoon ground black pepper
- 1 cup shredded sharp cheddar cheese, divided
- 1 cup shredded Colby Jack cheese, divided
- Vegetable oil, for greasing

INSTRUCTIONS
a) Preheat the oven to 350 degrees F.

b) In a large pan over medium heat, heat the oil. Add the Italian sausage, and cook until it browns. Toss in the onions and bell peppers. Cook until they soften.

c) Add the sour cream and cream cheese. Stir until well combined, then add the corn, green onion, jalapeño, garlic, and cilantro. Continue to stir the ingredients until everything is well incorporated. Sprinkle in the Creole seasoning, black pepper, ½ cup of cheddar, and ½ cup of Colby Jack cheese. Mix well.

d) Lightly grease a baking dish, then add in the corn mixture. Top with the remaining cheese and bake, uncovered, for 20 minutes. Cool slightly before serving.

76. Low-Carb pan pizza dip

Makes: 1 Serving

INGREDIENTS
- 6 oz. Cream Cheese microwaved
- 1/4 cup Sour Cream
- 1/2 cup Mozzarella Cheese, shredded
- Salt and Pepper to Taste
- 1/4 cup Mayonnaise
- 1/2 cup Mozzarella Cheese, shredded
- 1/2 cup Low-Carb Tomato Sauce
- 1/4 cup Parmesan Cheese

INSTRUCTIONS
a) Preheat the oven to 350 degrees Fahrenheit.
b) Mix the cream cheese, sour cream, mayonnaise, mozzarella salt and pepper.
c) Pour into ramekins and spread Tomato Sauce over each ramekin as well as mozzarella cheese and parmesan cheese.
d) Top your pan pizza dips with your favorite toppings.
e) Bake for 20 minutes.
f) Serve alongside some tasty breadsticks or pork rinds!

77. Crab rangoon dip

INGREDIENTS

f) 1 (8-ounce) package cream cheese, softened to room temperature
g) 2 tablespoons olive oil mayonnaise
h) 1 tablespoon freshly squeezed lemon juice
i) 1/2 teaspoon sea salt
j) 1/4 teaspoon black pepper
k) 2 cloves garlic, minced
l) 2 medium green onions, diced
m) 1/2 cup shredded Parmesan cheese
n) 4 ounces (about 1/2 cup) canned white crabmeat

INSTRUCTIONS

a) Preheat oven to 350°F.
b) In a medium bowl, mix cream cheese, mayonnaise, lemon juice, salt, and pepper with a hand blender until well incorporated.
c) Add garlic, onions, Parmesan cheese, and crabmeat and fold into mixture with a spatula.
d) Transfer mixture to an oven-safe crock and spread out evenly.
e) Bake 30–35 minutes until top of dip is slightly browned. Serve warm.

78. Goat Cheese Guacamole

Makes: 4-6

INGREDIENTS
- 2 avocados
- 3 ounces goat cheese
- zest from 2 limes
- lemon juice from 2 limes
- ¾ teaspoon garlic powder
- ¾ teaspoon onion powder
- ½ teaspoon salt
- ¼ teaspoon red pepper flakes (optional)
- ¼ teaspoon pepper

INSTRUCTIONS
- Add avocados to a food processor and blend until smooth. Add rest of **INGREDIENTS** and blend until incorporated.
- Serve with chips.

79. Bavarian party dip/spread

Makes: 1 1/4 pound

INGREDIENTS
- ½ cup Onions, minced
- 1 pounds Braunschweiger
- 3 ounces Cream cheese
- ¼ teaspoon Black pepper

INSTRUCTIONS
a) Sauté the onions 8-10 minutes, stirring frequently; remove from heat and drain. Remove the casing from Braunschweiger and mix meat with the cream cheese until smooth. Mix in onions and pepper.

b) Serve as a liver spread on crackers, thinly sliced party rye or serve as a dip accompanied by a variety of fresh raw vegetables like carrots, celery, broccoli, radishes, cauliflower or cherry tomatoes.

.

80. Baked artichoke party dip

INGREDIENTS
- 1 Loaf large dark rye bread
- 2 tablespoons Butter
- 1 bunch Green onions; chopped
- 6 Cloves of fresh garlic; minced finely, up to 8
- 8 ounces Cream cheese; at room temp.
- 16 ounces Sour cream
- 12 ounces Shredded cheddar cheese
- 1 can (14 oz.) artichoke hearts; drained and cut into quarters

INSTRUCTIONS
- Cut a hole in the top of the bread loaf about 5 inches in diameter. Remove soft bread from cut portion and discard. Reserve crust to make top for loaf.
- Scoop out most of the soft inside portion of the loaf and save for other purposes, such as stuffing or dried bread crumbs. In the butter,
- Sauté the green onions and the garlic until the onions wilt. Cut the cream cheese into small chunks, add the onions, garlic, sour cream and cheddar cheese. Mix well. Fold in artichoke hearts, Out all of this mixture into hollowed out bread. Place top on bread and wrap in a **HEAVY** duty aluminium foil. Bake in 350 degree oven for 1½ hours.
- When ready, remove foil and serve, using cocktail rye bread to dip out the sauce.

81. Buffalo chicken dip

INGREDIENTS
- 1 (8-ounce) package cream cheese
- 1/2 cup Frank's Red-Hot sauce
- 1/4 cup full-fat canned coconut milk
- 1 1/2 cups shredded cooked chicken
- 3/4 cup shredded mozzarella cheese, divided
- 1/2 cup blue cheese crumbles

INSTRUCTIONS
a) Add cream cheese to a medium saucepan and heat over medium-low heat until melted. Stir in hot sauce and coconut milk.
b) When combined, add chicken until heated through.
c) Remove from heat and stir in 1/2 cup mozzarella cheese and blue cheese crumbles.
d) Transfer to an 8" × 8" baking dish and sprinkle remaining mozzarella cheese on top. Bake 15 minutes or until cheese is bubbly. Serve warm.

82. <u>Ranch dip</u>

INGREDIENTS
- 1 cup mayonnaise
- 1/2 cup plain Greek yogurt
- 1 1/2 teaspoons dried chives
- 1 1/2 teaspoons dried parsley
- 1 1/2 teaspoons dried dill
- 3/4 teaspoon granulated garlic
- 3/4 teaspoon granulated onion
- 1/2 teaspoon salt
- 1/4 teaspoon black pepper

INSTRUCTIONS
a) Combine all ingredients in a small bowl.
b) Allow to sit in the refrigerator 30 minutes before serving.

83. **<u>Spicy shrimp and cheese dip</u>**

INGREDIENTS
- 2 slices no-sugar-added bacon
- 2 medium yellow onions, peeled and diced
- 2 cloves garlic, minced
- 1 cup popcorn shrimp (not the breaded kind), cooked
- 1 medium tomato, diced
- 3 cups shredded Monterey jack cheese
- 1/4 teaspoon Frank's Red-hot sauce
- 1/4 teaspoon cayenne pepper
- 1/4 teaspoon black pepper

INSTRUCTIONS
- Cook the bacon in a medium skillet over medium heat until crisp, about 5–10 minutes. Keep grease in pan. Lay the bacon on a paper towel to cool. When cool, crumble the bacon with your fingers.
- Add the onion and garlic to the bacon drippings in the skillet and sauté over medium-low heat until they are soft and fragrant, about 10 minutes.
- Combine all the ingredients in a slow cooker; stir well. Cook covered on low setting 1–2 hours or until cheese is fully melted.

84. Garlic and bacon dip

INGREDIENTS
- 8 slices no-sugar-added bacon
- 2 cups chopped spinach
- 1 (8-ounce) package cream cheese, softened
- 1/4 cup full-fat sour cream
- 1/4 cup plain full-fat Greek yogurt
- 2 tablespoons chopped fresh parsley
- 1 tablespoon lemon juice
- 6 cloves roasted garlic, mashed
- 1 teaspoon salt
- 1/2 teaspoon black pepper
- 1/2 cup grated Parmesan cheese

INSTRUCTIONS
- Preheat oven to 350°F.
- Cook bacon in a medium skillet over medium heat until crispy. Remove bacon from pan and set aside on a plate lined with paper towels.
- Add spinach to hot pan and cook until wilted. Remove from heat and set aside.
- To a medium bowl, add cream cheese, sour cream, yogurt, parsley, lemon juice, garlic, salt, and pepper and beat with a handheld mixer until combined.
- Roughly chop bacon and stir into cream cheese mixture. Stir in spinach and Parmesan cheese.
- Transfer to an 8" × 8" baking pan and bake 30 minutes or until hot and bubbly.

85. Creamy Goat Cheese Pesto Dip

INGREDIENTS
- 2 cups packed fresh basil leaves
- ½ cup grated parmesan cheese
- 8 ounces goat cheese
- 1-2 teaspoons minced garlic
- ½ teaspoon salt
- ½ cup olive oil

INSTRUCTIONS
- Mix basil, cheeses, garlic and salt in a food processor or blender until smooth. Add olive oil in even stream and mix until combined
- Serve immediately or store in refrigerator.

86. <u>Hot Pizza Super dip</u>

INGREDIENTS
- Softened Cream Cheese
- Mayonnaise
- Mozzarella Cheese
- Basil
- Oregano
- Garlic Powder
- Pepperoni
- Black Olives
- Green Bell Peppers

INSTRUCTIONS

a) Mix in your softened cream cheese, mayonnaise and a little bit of mozzarella cheese. Add a sprinkle of basil, oregano, parsley and garlic powder, stir until its nicely combined.

b) Fill it in to your deep dish pie plate and spread it out in an even layer.

c) Spread your pizza sauce on top and add your preferred toppings. For this example, we will add mozzarella cheese, pepperoni black olives and green peppers. Bake at 350 for 20 minutes.

87. <u>Baked Spinach and Artichoke Dip</u>

INGREDIENTS

a) 14 oz can un-marinated artichoke hearts, drained and coarsely chopped
b) 10 oz frozen chopped spinach thawed
c) 1 cup real mayo
d) 1 cup grated parmesan cheese
e) 1 garlic clove pressed

INSTRUCTIONS

- Thaw frozen spinach then squeeze it dry with your hands.
- Stir together: drained and chopped artichoke, squeezed spinach, 1 cup mayo, 3/4 cup parmesan cheese, 1 pressed garlic clove and transfer to a 1-quart casserole or pie dish. Sprinkle on remaining 1/4 cup parmesan cheese.
- Bake uncovered for 25 minutes at 350°F or until heated through. Serve with your favorite crostini, chips, or crackers.

88. Artichoke Dip

MAKES 8

INGREDIENTS
- 2 cups of artichoke hearts, chopped
- 1 cup mayonnaise or light mayonnaise
- 1 cup shredded Parmesan

INSTRUCTIONS
a) Combine all the ingredients, and place the mixture in a greased baking dish. Bake for 30 minutes at 350 °F.
b) Bake the dip until it is lightly browned and bubbly on top.

89. Creamy artichoke dip

INGREDIENTS
90. 2 x 8 oz. packages of cream cheese, room temp
91. 1/3 cup sour cream
92. 1/4 cup mayonnaise
93. 1 tablespoon lemon juice
94. 1 tablespoon Dijon mustard
95. 1 garlic clove
96. 1 teaspoon Worcestershire sauce
97. 1/2 teaspoon hot pepper sauce
98. 3 x 6 oz. jars marinated artichoke hearts, drained and chopped
99. 1 cup grated mozzarella cheese
100. 3 scallions
101. 2 teaspoon minced jalapeño

INSTRUCTIONS
- Using an electric mixer beat the first 8 **INGREDIENTS** in a large bowl until blended. Fold in artichokes, mozzarella, scallions, and jalapeño.
- Transfer to a baking dish.
- Preheat the oven to 400 °F.
- Bake dip until bubbling and brown on top— about 20 minutes.

90. Dill & Cream Cheese Dip

Makes: 4 to 6 servings

INGREDIENTS
- 1 cup plain soy yogurt
- 4 ounces Cream Cheese
- 1 tablespoon lemon juice
- 2 tablespoons dried chives
- 2 tablespoons dried dill weed
- 1/2 teaspoon sea salt
- Dash pepper

INSTRUCTIONS
a)   Blend everything and refrigerate for at least one hour.
NUTRITION: Calories 120| Fat 9g (Saturated 2g) | Cholesterol 0mg| Sodium 435mg| Carbohydrate 9g| Dietary Fiber 1g| Protein 3g.

91. Wild rice and Chili Dip

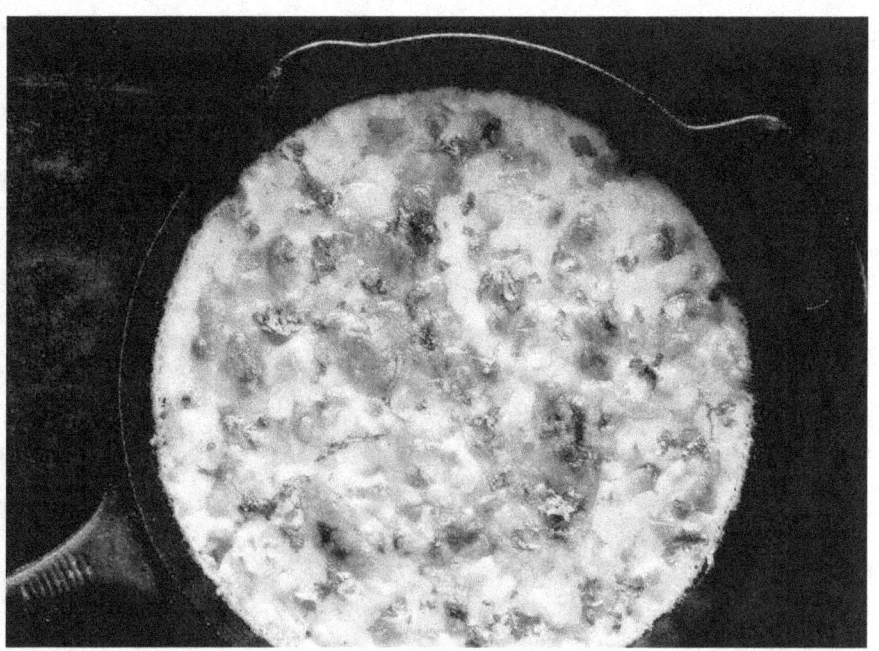

Makes: 4 to 6 servings

INGREDIENTS
- 12 ounces of cooked lentils
- 1/4 cup yeast-free vegetable broth
- 1/4 cup chopped green bell pepper
- 1/2 clove garlic, pressed
- 1 cup diced tomatoes
- 1/4 cup chopped onion
- 2 ounces Cream Cheese
- 1/2 tablespoon chili powder
- 1/2 teaspoon cumin
- 1/4 teaspoon sea salt
- Dash paprika
- 1/2 cup cooked wild rice

INSTRUCTIONS

a) In a small sauce pan, cook the lentils and vegetable broth.

b) Add the onions, bell pepper, garlic, and tomatoes and cook for 8 minutes over medium heat.

c) In a blender, combine Cream Cheese, chili powder, cumin, and sea salt until smooth.

d) Combine the rice, cream cheese blend, and lentil vegetable mix in a large mixing bowl and toss well.

92. <u>**Spicy Pumpkin & Cream Cheese Dip**</u>

Makes: 4 to 6 servings

INGREDIENTS
- 8 ounces Cream Cheese
- 15 ounces unsweetened canned pumpkin
- 1 teaspoon cinnamon
- 1/4 teaspoon allspice
- 1/4 teaspoon nutmeg
- 10 pecans, smashed

INSTRUCTIONS

a)   Whip the Cream Cheese and canned pumpkin together in a mixer until creamy.

b)   Stir in the cinnamon, allspice, nutmeg, and pecans until thoroughly combined. Before serving, chill for one hour in the refrigerator.

93. <u>**Cream Cheese and Honey Dip**</u>

Makes: 2 servings

INGREDIENTS
- 2 ounces Cream Cheese
- 2 tablespoons honey
- 1/4 cup squeezed orange juice
- 1/2 teaspoon ground cinnamon

INSTRUCTIONS
a) Blend everything until smooth.

94. Creamy Spinach-Tahini Dip

Makes about 1 cup

INGREDIENTS
- 1 (10-ounce) package fresh baby spinach
- 1 to 2 garlic cloves
- 1/2 teaspoon salt
- 1/3 cup tahini (sesame paste)
- Juice of 1 lemon
- Ground cayenne
- 2 teaspoons toasted sesame seeds, for garnish

INSTRUCTIONS
- Lightly steam the spinach until wilted, about 3 minutes. Squeeze dry and set aside.
- In a food processor, process the garlic and salt until finely chopped. Add the steamed spinach, tahini, lemon juice, and cayenne to taste.
- Process until well blended and taste, adjusting seasonings necessary.
- Transfer the dip to a medium bowl and sprinkle with the sesame seeds. If not using right away, cover and refrigerate until needed.
- Properly stored, it will keep for up to 3 days.

95. <u>Apricot And Chile Dipping Sauce</u>

Makes about 1 cup

INGREDIENTS
- 4 dried apricots
- 1/2 cup white grape juice or apple juice
- 1/2 teaspoon Asian chili paste
- 1/2 teaspoon grated fresh ginger
- 1 tablespoon soy sauce
- 1 tablespoon rice vinegar

INSTRUCTIONS
- In a small saucepan, combine the apricots and grape juice and heat just to a boil. Remove from the heat and set aside for 10 minutes to allow the apricots to soften.
- Transfer the apricot mixture to a blender or food processor and process until smooth. Add the chili paste, ginger, soy sauce, and vinegar and process until smooth. Taste, adjusting seasonings if necessary.
- Transfer to a small bowl. If not using right away, cover and refrigerate until needed.
- Properly stored, the sauce will keep for 2 to 3 days.

96. Roasted Eggplant Dip

Makes: 5 CUPS (1.19 L)

INGREDIENTS
- 3 medium eggplants with skin (the large, round, purple variety)
- 2 tablespoons oil
- 1 heaping teaspoon cumin seeds
- 1 teaspoon ground coriander
- 1 teaspoon turmeric powder
- 1 large yellow or red onion, peeled and diced
- 1 (2-inch [5-cm]) piece ginger root, peeled and grated or minced
- 8 cloves garlic, peeled and grated or minced
- 2 medium tomatoes, peeled (if possible) and diced
- 1–4 green Thai, serrano, or cayenne chiles, chopped
- 1 teaspoon red chile powder or cayenne
- 1 tablespoon coarse sea salt

INSTRUCTIONS
a) Set an oven rack at the second-highest position. Preheat the broiler to 500°F (260°C). Line a baking sheet with aluminum foil to avoid a mess later.

b) Poke holes in the eggplant with a fork (to release steam) and place them on the baking sheet. Broil for 30 minutes, turning once. The skin will be charred and burnt in some areas when they are done. Remove the baking sheet from the oven and let the eggplant cool for at least 15 minutes. With a sharp knife, and cut a split lengthwise from one end of each eggplant to the other, and pull it open slightly. Scoop out the roasted flesh inside, being careful to avoid the steam and salvage as much juice as possible. Place the roasted eggplant flesh in a bowl—you'll have about 4 cups (948 mL).

c) In a deep, heavy pan, heat the oil over medium-high heat.
d) Add the cumin and cook until it sizzles, about 30 seconds.
e) Add the coriander and turmeric. Mix and cook for 30 seconds.
f) Add the onion and brown for 2 minutes.
g) Add the ginger root and garlic and cook for 2 more minutes.
h) Add the tomatoes and chiles. Cook for 3 minutes, until the mixture softens.
i) Add the flesh from the roasted eggplants and cook for another 5 minutes, mixing occasionally to avoid sticking.
j) Add the red chile powder and salt. At this point, you should also remove and discard any stray pieces of charred eggplant skin.
k) Blend this mixture using an immersion blender or in a separate blender. Don't overdo it—there should still be some texture. Serve with toasted naan slices, crackers, or tortilla chips. You can also serve it traditionally with an Indian meal of roti, lentils, and raita.

97. Radish Microgreen & Lime Dip

INGREDIENTS

- 4 oz radish microgreens
- 2 oz cilantro
- 8 oz sour cream
- 1 TBSP yellow onion, grated
- 1 small clove garlic, grated
- 2 TBSP lime juice or to taste
- salt to taste
- red pepper flakes to taste

INSTRUCTIONS

- In a blender, combine microgreens, cilantro (stems and all), onion, garlic, and sour cream until smooth.

- Season with lime juice, salt, and a pinch of red pepper flakes. Serve with chips, vegetables, grilled meats, and other side dishes.

98. Mango-Ponzu Dipping Sauce

Makes about 1 1/4 cups

INGREDIENTS
d) 1 cup diced ripe mango
e) 1 tablespoon ponzu sauce
f) 1/4 teaspoon Asian chili paste
g) 1/4 teaspoon sugar
h) 2 tablespoons water, plus more if needed

INSTRUCTIONS
- In a blender or food processor, combine all the ingredients and blend until smooth, adding another tablespoon of water if a thinner sauce is desired.
- Transfer to a small bowl. Serve immediately or cover and refrigerate until ready to use. This sauce is best used on the same day it is made.

99. Eggplant Walnut Spread

Makes about 2 1/2 cups

INGREDIENTS
- 2 tablespoons olive oil
- 1 small onion, chopped
- 1 small eggplant, peeled and cut into 1/2-inch dice
- 2 garlic cloves, chopped
- 1/2 teaspoon salt
- 1/8 teaspoon ground cayenne
- 1/2 cup chopped walnuts
- 1 tablespoon fresh minced basil
- 2 tablespoons vegan mayonnaise
- 2 tablespoons chopped fresh parsley, for garnish

INSTRUCTIONS
a) In a large skillet, heat the oil over medium heat. Add the onion, eggplant, garlic, salt, and cayenne. Cover and cook until soft, about 15 minutes. Stir in the walnuts and basil and set aside to cool.
b) Transfer the cooled eggplant mixture to a food processor. Add the mayonnaise and process until smooth. Taste, adjusting seasonings if necessary, and then transfer to a medium bowl and garnish with the parsley.
c) If not using right away, cover and refrigerate until needed.
d) Properly stored, it will keep for up to 3 days.

100. Sassy Spinach Dip With Roasted Garlic

Makes about 2 1/2 cups

INGREDIENTS
- 5 to 7 garlic cloves
- 1 (10-ounce) package frozen chopped spinach, thawed
- 1/2 cup vegan mayonnaise, homemade (see Vegan Mayonnaise) or store-bought
- 1/2 cup vegan sour cream, homemade (see Tofu Sour Cream) or store-bought
- 2 teaspoons fresh lime juice
- 1/4 cup minced green onions
- 1/4 cup shredded carrot
- 2 tablespoons minced fresh cilantro or parsley
- 1/2 teaspoon celery salt
- Salt and freshly ground black pepper

INSTRUCTIONS
a) Preheat the oven to 350° F. Roast the garlic on a small baking sheet until golden, 12 to 15 minutes. Press or crush the roasted garlic and mash to a paste. Set aside.
b) While the garlic is roasting, steam the spinach until tender, 5 minutes. Squeeze dry and finely chop. Set aside.
c) In a medium bowl, combine the mayonnaise, sour cream, lime juice, and roasted garlic. Stir to combine. Add the green onions, carrot, and cilantro. Stir in the steamed spinach and season with the celery salt and salt and pepper to taste. Mix well. Chill at least 1 hour before serving to allow flavors to intensify. If not using right away, cover and refrigerate. Properly stored, it will keep for up to 3 days.

CONCLUSION

Nacho is a versatile and delicious dish that can be enjoyed by everyone. Whether you are a vegetarian or a meat lover, there is a nacho recipe for everyone. So, the next time you are in the mood for a snack, whip up a batch of nachos and enjoy the perfect combination of crunchy chips, melted cheese, and flavorful toppings.

www.ingramcontent.com/pod-product-compliance
Lightning Source LLC
LaVergne TN
LVHW021708060526
838200LV00050B/2559